THE ALNWICK BRANCH

Bartle Rippon

Kestrel Railway Books
PO Box 269
SOUTHAMPTON
SO30 4XR

www.kestrelrailwaybooks.co.uk

Printed by The Amadeus Press

ISBN 978-1-905505-11-1

Front cover: *One of a series of carriage prints used by the LNER around 1930. This is SD Badmin's print looking south towards Alnmouth village to the left and (hidden behind a hill, but indicated by the plume of smoke) the station on the right. Stephenson's "Eighteen Arches" viaduct is prominent in the foreground. (Bartle Rippon Collection)*

Title page: *Fletcher class 901 2-4-0 No 848 stands in Alnmouth's up platform awaiting departure with a southbound train to Newcastle around the turn of the century. (Bartle Rippon Collection)*

Dedication

To my wife, Judy, and our children, Nicola, Michael and Philippa for the many happy memories of our visits to Alnmouth station and surrounding area.

Contents

Acknowledgements

My thanks go to the staff at the National Archives at Kew, the record office at Woodhorn, Northumberland, the libraries of Alnwick and Amble, and the Ken Hoole Study Centre, Darlington Railway Museum.

All photographic copyright holders have been extensively sought, and apologies are given for any that have not been successfully located.

Thanks for advice and information go to John Addyman who has "rerailed" me from time to time, Jim Beverley, David Champion, John Horne, Keith McNally, Ken Middlemist, John Newbegin, William Stafford, Duncan Wilcock, Chris Woolstenholme, The Aln Valley Railway Society and Barter Books.

I would especially like to thank my wife, Judy, for her years of continued support with my interest in railways, the many hours of trekking around railway sites, the numerous visits to Alnmouth station and area, and the unenviable task of proof-reading this work.

The publishers would like to thank Steve Hughes of Retina Design for his assistance with the artwork for this book.

Bibliography:
The Alnwick and Cornhill Branch Line, John Addyman and John Mallon
The Amble Branch, Bartle Rippon
Clinker's Register of Closed Passenger Stations, CR Clinker
Gas in Alnwick, DP Dalby
George and Robert Stephenson, LTC Rolt
Locoshed Books, Ian Allan (various volumes)
Lost Railways of Northumberland, Robert Kinghorn
North East Diaries, 1939 to 1945, Ripley and Pears
North East Locomotive Sheds, Ken Hoole
North Eastern Branch Line Termini, Ken Hoole
A Portrait of Northumberland, Nancy Ridley
Rail Tales and Station Stories, CD produced by Barter Books
Railways of Northumberland, Alan Young
The *Railways of Northumberland* series, CR Warn
The Xpress Locomotive Register, Vol 3: E, NE, & Sc Regions, Xpress Publications

Introduction

Alnwick, the county town of Northumberland and the seat of the Duke of Northumberland, has been noted throughout history for its northerly importance. Situated in England's border country, where took place many a battle between the English and the Scots, Alnwick Castle stood witness over the fighting armies of years gone by.

Mention of Alnwick recalls the Percy family, Harry Hotspur and visits from royalty, as well as the more modern day location of "adventure" film-making and the even more recent visit of the magical Harry Potter!

Alnwick was never to have the status of a main line station because of its geographical position, but eventually a branch line made its way to the town and a majestic terminus was constructed. This short branch line, only three miles in length, was connected to the main line at the present-day Alnmouth station – previously named Bilton.

Alnmouth station, situated approximately half-way between Newcastle and Berwick, and a little over a mile from the coast, was built to serve the town of Alnwick and its surrounding area. It is here that most locomotive activity (the greatest interest to the railway enthusiast) occurred. Alnmouth station boasted a sizeable engine shed, two small goods yards and a busy "station life".

The branch line offered coast-to-castle travel for just over one hundred years, with a fully steam-hauled passenger service operating until 1966, when workings were taken over by diesel multiple unit trains shortly before closure.

This history of the branch line from Alnmouth to Alnwick attempts to describe the life around the two stations, both as a memorial to early engineering and operation and also to the social development of two communities. It is also to share my enjoyment and appreciation of a wonderful location, which holds very many fond memories for me.

I have enjoyed train-spotting at Alnmouth for many years, fully appreciating the beauty of the area. From Alnmouth station's platforms, I have witnessed a great variety of steam and diesel locomotives, also finding the railway people just as interesting as the trains themselves. To go to Alnmouth, and sometimes Alnwick, was always a delight, and a pleasure that my family also shared.

Through reading this book, I hope you will experience some of the pleasures of the area. I have certainly enjoyed the pleasure of writing about it, and reliving those many happy occasions.

Bartle Rippon
Perth, Western Australia, 2008

Bart's previous book, *The Amble Branch*, is still available.
ISBN: 978-1-905505-05-0

The development of railways in Northumberland. On the left is the situation in 1854 with a line running from Lesbury (actually from a junction at Bilton) on the York, Newcastle & Berwick Railway to Alnwick. On the right, the map shows the North Eastern Railway at its zenith in 1922, and immediately before the Grouping. Lesbury is closed, Bilton Junction has been renamed Alnmouth, and the Alnwick to Cornhill (Coldstream) line has been completed.

Chapter 2

Alnmouth Station

Sitting on the main Newcastle to Edinburgh line, some thirty-five miles north of Newcastle and just over a mile from the coast, Alnmouth Station was the junction for all trains to Alnwick, the County town of Northumberland. Not only did Alnmouth station serve the town of Alnwick, it also provided access to the communities of the Lesbury and Alnmouth areas and, in later years, those of Amble and RAF Boulmer. However, despite being in use since 1850, it was not to be known as Alnmouth station until some forty years later, nor was it the first station to serve this area.

When the main line opened in 1847, there were no station facilities at Alnmouth nor a branch line to Alnwick. To appease the people of Alnwick and the Duke of Northumberland, the York, Newcastle and Berwick Railway originally provided station facilities by building the little-remembered Lesbury Station about three miles away from the town in 1847. Shortly afterwards, with the opening of the three-mile, double-track branch line to Alnwick in 1850, Lesbury station was superseded by a new station which became the principal station in the area. This new station was a three-platform junction with goods sidings and an engine shed. For over forty years it was known as Bilton station,

before eventually becoming officially known as Alnmouth Station in 1892.

Lesbury Station 1847–1851

The first station in the Alnmouth area, Lesbury Station, opened in 1847, coinciding with the opening of the Newcastle to Berwick railway. It lasted approximately four years until it officially closed to passenger and goods traffic in April 1851, although it might have unofficially closed earlier. Lesbury's brief spell as a station occurred when it was built to serve the people of Alnwick, who had unsuccessfully petitioned for the railway to pass through their town, and in 1850, when the branch line to Alnwick opened, it became redundant as all services and train connections were transferred to the newly-constructed Bilton station.

Lesbury station was one of Benjamin Green's designs, and was at the north end of Robert Stephenson's viaduct over the River Aln, known locally as the "Eighteen Arches". Although the old station house still remains today, there is no trace of the station platforms or goods dock (if it ever had one). The station was situated near the main road, later to be

The original station house at Lesbury Station that was briefly the station for Alnwick before Bilton (later Alnmouth) was built. This 1953 view shows is all that is left. No trace of the platforms can be seen. (William Stafford)

classed as the A1068, leading to Alnwick. This was the nearest station that the Alnwick townsfolk and its Duke could use until the branch line into Alnwick itself came into operation.

Reid's monthly timetables of May 1849 show six trains calling each day in both directions at Lesbury. On Sundays there were three trains stopping northbound and four southbound.

The station had the distinction of a visit by Queen Victoria on her journey north to officially open the Royal Border Bridge at Berwick. The people of the borough of Alnmouth invited the Queen to stop at Lesbury station and receive a "…humble address from this ancient borough to her Majesty Queen Victoria on her passage through this parish". It was delivered amid a tide of excitement at 2pm on 29th August 1850. Apparently the welcome address was more like a lecture on how to run the country, according to the "Record of Proceedings" as mentioned in Nancy Ridley's book *Portrait of Northumberland.*

The viaduct is another fine example of Victorian engineering, with its eighteen arches each of thirty foot spans. Built of stone, the viaduct straddles the River Aln and the deeply-eroded river bed.

As Bilton station, to the south of the viaduct, was in use by 1850, and the Government Census of 1851 states that the station building at Lesbury was uninhabited, it can be assumed that Lesbury Station was no longer in use by 1851.

After the official closure of Lesbury the station house was split into two dwellings for railway employees, and remained that way until the late 1950s, when it was converted back into

"Eighteen Arches" viaduct, over the River Aln, now with overhead line equipment, seen (top) in 1998, and (above) viewed from Alnmouth station on 2nd June 2006. (Bartle Rippon and Howard Sprenger/Kestrel Collection)

In about 1920, an Alnwick to Newcastle train prepares to leave with locomotive 1504 in charge. The locomotive does not provide much protection from the weather for its crew. Passengers are waiting on the down platform for a northbound train, while those wonderful enamel advert signs for OXO, Andrew's Liver Salts and Sunlight Soap adorn the up platform. Hanging from the canopy of the down platform roof is a Refreshment Room sign. (Ken Nunn Collection)

a single house. Brick-built sheds were added to the site around the end of the 1890s or early 1900s, the bricks being stamped with the NER initials, and dated 1897.

The 1901 census records Mr Charles Gesting, aged 49, a railway inspector and Mr John Putton, aged 30, a railway labourer, as living in the "Old Station" at Lesbury. The station house still remains today, and is still lived in.

Bilton Station 1850–1892

Bilton station lay in a cutting that opened out into undulating land and was therefore not visible from the main road. Travelling up the bank from Hipsburn towards Shilbottle, the first opportunity of seeing the station was a fleeting glance to the right before passing over the road bridge, and immediately before the bridge, a connecting road to the right appeared and led down to the station area.

There were three platforms, the two main ones for passengers for north- and south-bound trains, and a third one for the sole use of the branch passenger train that serviced the Duke of Northumberland's seat of Alnwick.

The principal buildings and rooms were on the up side of the railway on the east side of the site, although some conveniences and minor rooms were situated on the island platform. Unfortunately, no details have been found as to the cost and exact date of building of Bilton station, or by whom

it was actually constructed. However, an Ordnance Survey map of 1860 depicts three buildings making up the station buildings along with those on the island platform.

Small extensions were added in later years in the form of a refreshment room, a yard foreman's office and a bookstall, but eventually these became defunct. The station buildings, which included the station master's house, would remain unchanged until their demolition during the 1980s.

After some forty years, Bilton station was eventually renamed Alnmouth on 2nd May 1892. This was as a result of Alnmouth businessmen requesting that the railway company (now the NER) rename the station in order to help regenerate their ailing businesses and promote Alnmouth as a business centre.

At one time Alnmouth had eighteen granaries from which corn was exported, and also imported goods from Holland and wood from Norway; there had been a shipbuilding yard too. Alnmouth village ceased as a port after heavy storms in 1806 altered the course of the river mouth, thus preventing the berthing of many sea craft. Many local businesses gradually suffered, and failed from this adversity. However, the name change of the station seemed to make no direct difference to the village's prosperity, although eventually, due to its beautiful coastal location and the cheap rail travel being offered, tourism became a thriving industry. Alnmouth village now took on a different economic perspective.

Alnmouth Station from 1892

The station buildings had been designed on a low budget, and therefore lacked some of the fine architectural features used on this stretch of railway north of Newcastle such as at Warkworth and Acklington Stations. Most of the alterations occurring around the station area were signalling improvements, with two new signalboxes being built around 1907. The gasometer, or gasworks, shown on the 1860 OS map had disappeared by 1936.

Alnmouth South signalbox was removed in the early 1950s, and the Alnmouth area was again resignalled, this time to electric colour lights during 1963 and 1964. All semaphore signals and gantries were then removed. Some minor track alterations took place in 1962 when the double-slip crossover points at the north end of the down platform were taken out and replaced with a simpler cross-over point system. Gradually rationalisation of the station would take place, and all the original buildings would disappear, some being replaced with modern ones, and the platforms would be extended.

An Early 1960s View

During my early time visiting Alnmouth station, the entrance to the station from the forecourt was through an archway where, to the left, were the ticket office windows and, to the right, was an attractive tiled map of the NER network. Incorporated in the station buildings to the north end of the station was the station master's house with the water tank supplying the locomotives nearby.

There were several other buildings attached to, or associated with, the station. The station concourse itself consisted of the booking and parcels office, ladies' waiting room, general waiting room, station master's office, signal & telegraph rooms (marked "Private"), conveniences and a guards' room, which appeared to be a later wooden addition attached to the south end of the station buildings. The station master's house, being part of the station buildings, had access directly onto the station platform, but by the time I made my acquaintance with the station, the house was no longer used as a residence, being only storage rooms for railway equipment.

The heating in the passengers' waiting rooms was from a solitary stove; fuel was never a problem as there was always a

A 1907 view of Alnmouth station showing the signal box and engine shed. The signal box has recently been built as part of the resignalling scheme of the time, and a mass of points and trackwork fills the area. Standing on No 5 road, at the side of the engine shed, is an NER clerestory-roofed carriage. The station cottages stand proud above the end of the engine shed. (John Mallon Collection)

Top: Worsdell class D20 4-4-0 62355 is ready to leave Alnmouth's platform one with its train for Alnwick on 5th September 1955.

Bottom: The north end of Alnmouth station's island platform displaying the distinct signal gantry that straddled the main line. The house to the left used to be occupied by the Station Master. 5th September 1955. (Both HC Casserley)

The approach to Alnmouth station looking rather drab on a dull day during 1970. (Bartle Rippon)

plentiful supply of coal at the engine sheds. The rooms were always difficult to keep warm during the winter months as doors were constantly left open, but when there was little or no activity around the station it was delightful to sit around the stove keeping warm.

The décor always appeared drab, usually of brown, varnish-style coating and "mock" leather seating. The one bright spot on the station was the post box – a small box set into the stone wall on the up platform side of the main building. Painted in red, it bore the name of Victoria – a monument to the good queen and the Victorian period when the station was first built. Near to it was a steel drinking fountain.

Set a little away from the main station building towards the signalbox, but on the east side of the station, was the carriage and wagon office. Here were stored the necessary lubricants, etc, for the servicing of axle boxes for the rolling stock.

On the west side of the main railway lines was the island platform, accessible via a covered-in wooden footbridge (bridge No 107). The island platform not only served the trains travelling northwards to Berwick, Edinburgh and beyond, but the passenger service to Alnwick. To the west of the island platform, the area opened out into a small goods yard for transferring freight and the site of the locomotive shed.

The two main lines through the station allowed for trains to travel at speeds up to 60mph, which caused considerable draughts from the expresses as they appeared to "fly" through this confined area.

The Alnwick Train

I always enjoyed the arrival of the Alnwick train, watching the locomotive uncouple, run around its train and recouple again at the other end. This exercise meant moving out onto the main line, followed by a short run back to the down goods yard before moving forward to couple back onto the train; I was fortunate to enjoy being on the locomotive footplate on one occasion. Also, depending on who was the passenger guard of the Alnwick train, I often had the opportunity of changing the tail lamp from one end of the train to the other.

When the departure of the Alnwick train coincided with the departure of a northbound train, it was sometimes interesting to watch a "race" between the two trains out of the platforms. However, there was many an occasion when a late passenger would be rushing across the footbridge amid shouts from railway staff to hold the train; the "race" was foiled!

Between the Alnwick branch platform and the engine shed was the goods yard, a small five-road affair basically for shunting purposes and transferring wagons from one area to another. Wagons would be left by main line goods trains in these sidings before being forwarded to Alnwick or to the south goods yard for more local recipients. In the south goods yard where the goods shed and coal drops were situated, the local coal merchant collected the coal, bagged it, and delivered it. Also in the south yard was Alnmouth South signalbox, built around 1906. Unfortunately, details of its track diagram have proven difficult to obtain.

The locomotive shed was a rather substantial, two-track brick building, looking every bit as handsome as the station

"strange" locomotives visiting the area. USA 2-8-0 locomotives were observed during 1943 and 1944, as well as two ex-North British locomotives, class J36 No 9172 and class J37 No 9046. These latter locomotives spent some time at Alnmouth, and were frequently deployed on the Alnwick to Wooler goods trains.

On the CD *Rail Tales and Station Stories*, Edward Potts recalls reporting for his first evening duty on the 26th August 1942 and, with some enthusiasm, tells of being challenged by some Polish soldiers, "Halt! Who goes there?" Surprised, he duly answered that he was reporting for work at the engine shed, and then discovered that, standing inside the engine shed, under military guard, was a three-inch gun, along with machine guns, mounted on armour-plated rolling stock coupled to a guard's van. The driver and fireman were from the Royal Engineers, and apparently this unit travelled regularly between Berwick and Darlington where it was used for protection against enemy aircraft. It often stayed in the engine shed.

Another tale on the CD, relating to Alnmouth's celebrated LNER D17 (NER class M) locomotive 1621, first appeared as an article in *North Eastern Express*, February 1968, entitled *A War-Time Experience*:

During a war-time exercise in September 1944, Mr TE (Tom) Rounthwaite, along with other members of his company, was taking part in some strenuous infantry training while based at Felton. They were taken by lorry and left somewhere in Northumberland, then told to make their way home and instructed not to ask where they were. As there were no signposts (a wartime precaution to mislead an invading army) a vantage point was needed to survey the area. Finding one, all that could be located was the sea to one side and the sun in the south-west. There were few landmarks to help their situation, but far away was a smoking chimney, and what looked like colliery spoil heaps. Knowing there were some small collieries between Amble and Shilbottle, Tom knew that Felton was not far away, so when he told this to the others in his group he was promptly elected their leader!

After some two hours walking along the country lanes, the party came across a small overbridge spanning two railway tracks running through a cutting. The men debated in which direction they were walking and Tom's sense of direction began slipping slowly away. He knew this was not the east coast main line as the railway curved westwards up hill. Then, in the distance, a plume of steam was spotted. Rounding the bend towards the bridge the train come into view. The engine was one of the last pair of NER class M locomotives, and even better was the fact that Tom knew that this was the Alnmouth to Alnwick branch line. 'It should be No 1621', he told his companions, who were absolutely amazed at how correct he was. From that, he knew exactly where they were and soon had the men back at camp in Felton in record time!

Post-War Years

After World War II, Alnmouth and Alnwick had their share of visitors when several class Q6 0-8-0 locomotives arrived on ballast and cattle trains, and a WD 2-8-0 locomotive came with a sheep train. This latter type might not have been that uncommon, as Tweedmouth shed had a complement of about six at that time. The popular D20s were usefully employed around Alnmouth, Alnwick and the area, but by the end of the 1950s their days were running out, and they were replaced by class J39 0-6-0s, and eventually, K1 2-6-0s during the early 1960s.

There were occasions when other types of locomotive could be seen at Alnmouth shed. Class V3 2-6-2T locomotives 67656 and 67683 were there between May and June 1957, while class V1 locomotives, 67641, 67642 and 67647 spent some time there from November 1957 to June 1958, before returning to Heaton shed in Newcastle. The bigger V2 2-6-2s could also be seen around the area, such as 60836 and 60846 of St. Margaret's shed in Edinburgh (64A).

Class V2 60836, based at Dundee and eventually to become the last V2 in regular British Railways service, spent several months at Alnmouth during 1965. Ken Middlemist, one of Alnmouth's firemen, recalls its presence, having taken a K1 to Tweedmouth for repair, and brought back this locomotive as the replacement. It was used regularly on the Alnwick Branch passenger train and even travelled to Amble with a load of Shilbottle coal for export, where it was photographed by me on 27th May 1966.

This V2 2-6-2 locomotive was not the only one of its kind to be used at Alnmouth, as there had been many instances of the same locomotive class visiting over a period of time. On one occasion not only did I photograph V2 60846, but I was also taken by one of the shed staff for a look around it. Climbing into the cab of the locomotive, and looking at what seemed a spacious footplate, as well as all the shining pipes and gauges in front of me, was quite an experience. It was explained briefly how things worked, but the fascination of just being on the footplate was enough. I was then taken down into the pit for a look underneath the locomotive. It was an incredible sight to see the third piston and all the workings underneath, and I quickly learnt how low a person had to bend and be watchful of both dripping water and oil. I was not taken the full length of the locomotive as that would have meant going under the firebox!

Whilst being on this tour I could hear an express train of some kind passing through the station. Although I wished I could have recorded the locomotive's number, it was not as much fun as being where I was. The only sad part of the visit was not being able to photograph the event, as my camera (a Brownie 127) was never equipped to take flash photography!

The V2 locomotive was a frequent visitor to Alnmouth, often coming from Tweedmouth, and an earlier occasion recorded the visit of a V2 locomotive to Alnwick via Alnmouth. It happened in 1953, when a Coronation Pageant excursion worked its way from Newcastle to Alnwick on 5th June, hauled by class V2 2-6-2 No 60949, a Gateshead

Class K1 2-6-0 No 62021 stands outside the engine shed in 1965 in front of another unidentified member of the same class. (Bartle Rippon)

The sun streams down on class K1 2-6-0 No 62028 in October 1965, an unusual visitor to Alnmouth shed, but there to replace a fellow member of the same class that had probably gone away for repairs. (Bartle Rippon)

engine. At Alnwick the turntable was not big enough, nor was there any other means for it to turn and face the correct way for the return journey, so the locomotive had to travel to Tweedmouth to be turned, and return to Alnwick in time for the departure.

Although the passenger service to Alnwick was still very much in evidence, goods traffic principally became the movement of coal from Shilbottle exchange sidings and Whittle Colliery's South Side sidings near Warkworth. There were still the local pick-up goods trains that ran when required, but much of the traffic was being lost to road transport. A regular train working of coal for the cement works at Oxwellmains, Dunbar, in the Scottish Borders, was one of the turns for Alnmouth locomotives and staff.

Ken Middlemist recalls many tales about the journeys to Oxwellmains firing a K1 locomotive, where he could always get up a good head of steam to take the train northwards, but the return journey sometimes posed a problem. Having got to Oxwellmains the locomotive would turn around at Dunbar in readiness to collect an empty train of coal hoppers to be brought back. Steaming the locomotive became far more difficult on the return journey, as the coal at the bottom of the tender was not as good as the "fresh" coal that had recently been loaded, much of it having broken down to dust. This made it difficult to keep a good fire and create steam up to the required pressure.

There was the occasion during 1962 when the Anglo-Scottish car carrier's locomotive failed at Alnmouth. The locomotive was removed and replaced by one of Alnmouth's K1s, and apparently the pyrotechnic display out of the chimney was something to behold as it started to pull away with this heavy train. Having reached Newcastle, it went to Gateshead sheds to be serviced, and there the driver and fireman reported having to go over it tightening up every nut and bolt!

Ken also recalls his days as fireman having to go to Heaton, Newcastle, with a goods train, and return with a similar one around 9pm. Back at Alnmouth, it was time to shunt the wagons in preparation for their early morning onward journeys and then service his locomotive. This would mean filling it up with coal and water, making sure that the fire was free from clinker, ash, etc, and keeping the boiler pressure at an appropriate level. When these and the general cleaning jobs were done, it was then off to prepare other locomotives in a similar way for the following day. Often Ken and his colleague would remain at the shed should anyone have overslept and missed the start of their early morning shift; they were ready to take their place – as Ken always said, "This was team work!"

Ken Middlemist grew up at Hipsburn, and joined the railway at Alnmouth in his late teens as a cleaner, eventually becoming a fireman. Ken enjoyed his time firing and driving the locomotives, and working with his father who was an engine driver at the station. Although I had known Ken some years ago, it was not until our meeting during an AVRS social evening many years later that our acquaintance became renewed. He had on display a photograph showing me as a

boy photographing the same locomotive that he had photographed, V2 60955, but from the opposite side of the station. An eerie experience! *(See pages 3 and 4.)*

The final years of steam working from Alnmouth were in charge of several K1 locomotives, although from time to time other classes appeared. Class V2, class B1, BR class 3MT, BR class 2MT, and other K1s were the usual replacements, but not always at the same time. Locomotives noted were B1 61019, K1s 62002 and 62022, 2MTs 78024 and 78025, and 3MTs 77002 and 77004.

Not long before the end of steam at Alnmouth in June 1966, it appears that the majority of the K1s were being transferred away and other locomotives appeared in their places. There was an occasion during April 1966 when Stanier "Black 5" 44925 turned up on shed at Alnmouth. It had come from Edinburgh, St. Margaret's, possibly via Tweedmouth, but did not last long at all, and very quickly went back north again. It was after this that V2 60836 had its well-documented brief spell at Alnmouth. Around this time, I was informed that a Britannia locomotive, of Carlisle Shed (12A), heading a north-bound goods, had been seen taking water before continuing its journey – another of my missed opportunities.

Alnmouth Locomotive Allocations

December 1938: Class D20 4-4-0 1078, 2023, 2029, 2106.

August 1950: Class D20 4-4-0 62349, 62351, 62352, 62354, 62357, 62358, 62360, 62362, 62371, 62380, 62387.

January 1955: Class D20 4-4-0 62355, 63260, 62375, 62383; Class J39 0-6-0 64868, 64897, 64941.

November 1960: Class J39 0-6-0 64824, 64868, 64897, 64916, 64929, 64949.

January 1963: Class K1 2-6-0 62006, 62011, 62012, 62021, 62023, 62025.

January 1965: Class K1 2-6-0 62006, 62011, 62021, 62023, 62025, 62030.

June 1966 (final allocation): Class K1 2-6-0 62006, 62011, 62021, 62023, 62025, 62050.

18th June 1966 saw the last day of steam operation on the Alnwick Branch. The two principal locomotives used for the occasion were BR 9F 92099 and K1 62011. Ken Middlemist recalls his last working on the K1 with great relish, 62011 being his favourite locomotive. He had worked the morning shift, and returned to Alnmouth around lunchtime to sign off duty. He noticed standing at the shed a rather large BR 9F locomotive from Tyne Dock, South Shields, and this locomotive would now take over the passenger duty for the remainder of the day. Ken had been told that a 9F locomotive would be appropriate, as it was the last class of steam

Stanier class 5 4-6-0 No 44925, stands outside Alnmouth shed probably having arrived from Tweedmouth in exchange for a K1 locomotive needing mechanical attention, as was the usual practice. Having made its way south from St Margaret's shed, Edinburgh (probably with a goods train) it was used at Alnmouth for a short time, but when St. Margaret's shed realised its absence, it was quickly recalled to resume its work north of the border! This practice of locomotive exchange occurred quite often. (John Newbegin)

Class K1 2-6-0 No 62021 steams well outside the engine shed having just been coaled in around 1965. (DH Beecroft)

Standing in the late evening sunshine in February 1966, the rain has ceased, and rays of sunlight stream through the smoke and steam, cascading onto the engine sheds and platform. K1 2-6-0 No 62025 awaits passengers for Alnwick. (John Newbegin)

Alnmouth's class K1 62012 is about to leave the down yard with freight wagons for the up yard. Has anyone noticed that no lamps have been placed on the front of the locomotive? Certainly not the driver or fireman! This locomotive had not long arrived from its busy life at Fort William, where it spent several years operating on the West Highland Railway from Fort William to Mallaig. (Bartle Rippon)

locomotive built for the British Railways, *Evening Star* being the very last one. Ironically, I missed this special event, having been at work all day, and then having to attend a family engagement while the spectacle at Alnmouth was taking place!

The engine sheds officially closed to steam on Sunday 19th June 1966, and locomotives 62011, 62025 and 62050 were transferred to Blyth (52F) while locomotives 62006, 62021 and 62023 were transferred to Sunderland (52G). Several of these locomotives had already gone by the end.

Although the passenger services continued for a short while afterwards using diesel multiple units, the steam era for Alnmouth and Alnwick had come to an end. Along with the cottages at "Branch End", the engine shed was demolished by one man and his JCB or bulldozer during the spring of 1969. The rubble was removed in wagons as the sidings were still in use.

Diesel multiple units had been operating the Newcastle to Alnwick service since 1958, and even had their share of problems. In Alnmouth's signalbox register for Wednesday 26th August 1964, it was recorded that the afternoon passenger service, 2G78 from Newcastle, was experiencing motor troubles. At every station along the route, the driver had requested water to top up his radiator. The train still managed to arrive at Alnwick Station with little loss of time, but there are no indications to what happened regarding its return journey.

All the sidings in the down yard were lifted in 1973.

Left: The building for the Carriage & Wagon Department at the north end of the station seen here in 1969. The cables are for the signal & telecommunications operations, and the ivy is enjoying the aspect of the sun and creeping its way all over the south end of the building.

Below: Having spent a few months at Alnmouth, class K1 2-6-0 No 62050 has been spruced up and serviced ready for its next job in 1966. (Both Bartle Rippon)

Chapter 4

Alnmouth to Alnwick – "From Coast to Castle"

The Alnwick branch was the short railway link from the main line to the County Town, where two- and sometimes three-coach trains, always hauled by one of Alnmouth's several steam locomotives, were a wonderful sight to watch depart and return on a regular basis. This gave me the opportunity at a young age to stand alongside a steam locomotive, look into the cab, and watch whatever activity was going on. Then there was that smell of steam and oil, so reminiscent of the era!

I could not always afford the extra train fare to Alnwick, having already used my pocket money for the bus to Alnmouth Station, so I usually had to content myself with everything that happened at Alnmouth. I was always afraid that, should I go to Alnwick for the train ride, I might just miss an exciting event on the main line such as the passing of a steam locomotive! There was the odd occasion, however, when I did embark on this journey to meet my oldest brother in Alnwick market square, and then travel home by bus to Amble.

It was a lovely ride from Alnmouth to Alnwick, and more so in the diesel multiple units, as they gave a far greater view of the countryside, and sitting at the very front you had a driver's eye view of the journey. The diesel multiple units had been introduced in the very late 1950s as replacements for the steam-hauled passenger trains from Newcastle to Alnwick and return. The journey between the two stations was short both in distance and time, usually seven minutes for the uphill journey to Alnwick, and six on the downhill return to cover the three miles.

My personal journeys to Alnwick from Amble during the 1960s were always by bus because of the convenient nature of arriving almost in the centre of the town instead of the more laborious routine of changing at Hipsburn, walking to Alnmouth Station for the train, then alighting in Alnwick, and having to walk a reasonable distance to the town centre. Not having frequented Alnwick station as much as I did Alnmouth at that time, my knowledge of, and relationship with, Alnwick was therefore much less. Consequently, my own photographs rarely included Alnwick Station, which is now a matter of some regret to me.

The Branch to Alnwick

The branch line to Alnwick was a mere three miles in length, but needed quite an amount of engineering to create it. It had the distinction of being double-track for the entire route, something that was unusual for a line with branch status. It had three overbridges, eight cuttings of various lengths, and four underbridges, of which one was a fine seven-arch viaduct over the Cawledge Burn, which ran into the River Aln. Other evidence found on railway plans of 1936 states that there were actually ten bridges along the branch. Nowhere did the gradient ever exceed 1 in 77, rising as it

snaked its way towards Alnwick, entering the town from the south.

There had been three principal proposals in 1840 for the Newcastle to Edinburgh railway, but none of them was to include the town of Alnwick. When Stephenson first planned the Newcastle to Berwick section of the Great North British Railway to Edinburgh in 1839, it was intended to pass through Bedlington, the seaward side of Warkworth, much closer to the coast, and on the west side of Alnmouth village. Another proposal by a Mr Remington would take the line through Morpeth to Wooler, Kelso and Dalkeith, and a direct line by Malcolm Edmund Bowman via Morpeth was to join the Stephenson route north of Alnmouth. The Smith-Barlow Report of 1841 regarded the Remington line as totally unacceptable on engineering grounds, and when Lord Howick would not accept the intrusion of the railway line between his home, Howick Hall, and the sea, substantial alterations had to be made to Stephenson's alignment. Because of his influential powers, Brunel was invited to prepare his alternative proposal using atmospheric propulsion. Fortunately for the prospective shareholders, the Brunel Bill was defeated, but Stephenson was forced to accept steeper gradients, sharper curves and greater expense to overcome his lordship's objections.

The topography was against a direct railway from Morpeth to Alnwick. Using Telford's Great North Road levels, the Smith-Barlow Report stated that, after creating substantial cuttings and embankments, gradients would be steeper than 1 in 100. Just four miles south of Alnwick, the road is 350 feet higher than the present main line, and a falling gradient of 1 in 66 would be needed to enter Alnwick with a climb of 1 in 44 being necessary travelling northwards out of Alnwick. This explanation was completely different from that which I was always led to believe, namely that the Duke of Northumberland was alleged to have claimed that his lands and castle would be badly interfered with by the trains, and that he therefore refused access. It would have taken an earthquake, or even the wizardry of Harry Potter, to damage Alnwick Castle!

The Duke of Northumberland was petitioned by the Alnwick Railway Committee on 6th November 1844 to use his influence to prevent the railway avoiding the town. Through the Alnwick Railway Committee, the residents of the town held various public meetings, fearing that they would lose their livelihoods and that all local goods would be taken elsewhere, while the town would lose its status as a County Town if it were not on the main line. The Duke replied that eminent engineers had found difficulties in engineering a line to serve it, and that he felt that improvements to the road to Lesbury would suit him just as well as a branch line to the town. Having made no headway with His Grace, the Committee put its case to Lord Dalhousie, then President of the Board of Trade, who supported a branch from the main line to Alnwick, which

Stephenson then included in his plans. On 31st July 1845, an Act was passed giving the royal assent for the building of the Newcastle to Berwick main line, as well as the branch lines to Alnwick, Amble and Kelso.

Due to Lord Howick's objections, the Newcastle & Berwick Railway Company had to revise the earlier Stephenson route to pass to the west of Lesbury, making it slightly nearer to Alnwick. As we have seen, the original main line station to serve Alnwick and its townsfolk was built at Lesbury, but there was still a considerable distance of about three miles from the station to the town by road.

Although the Act for a branch to Alnwick had been granted on 31st July 1845, it was another three years before the Newcastle & Berwick Railway Company constructed it. Tenders were invited, and it was that from Rush and Lawton that was accepted on 8th August 1848 for the construction of the branch at a cost of £34,897. When work was completed, the branch line was opened for passengers on 18th August 1850, and for goods traffic on 1st October 1850.

Contracts for building the Alnwick Branch, 1850	
Thomas King, Morpeth	£33.886
Rush & Lawton	£34,897
Richard Cail	£35,990
William Hutchinson	£36,150
McKay & Blackstock	£37,264
Robert Norris	£39,849
Edmund Reed	£41,000
Hattersley & Nowell	£41,961
Wilson & Gibson	£42,758
Charles John Pearson, Gateshead	£53,900

The official point where the branch line began is 60ft south of the overbridge (bridge No 105), the location where the branch line joins the main line. From the Alnwick platform, the line left the north end of Bilton station, and proceeded level with the main line for about three-quarters of a mile before turning north-westwards, to pass "Branch End".

Heading towards Alnwick, the railway passed over a small bridge, where the local farmer had access between his fields, the route then passing through two cuttings and under a road bridge. This bridge was in the area of Greenrigg, and took the road down to Bilton Mill at the River Aln. The railway next encountered the brief, but spectacular view of the countryside around the Cawledge Burn as it passed over the viaduct. This viaduct was a shorter version of the attractive "Eighteen Arches" over the River Aln, also designed by Robert Stephenson. There were seven arches, each with a span of 45ft, and the viaduct was approximately 53ft at its highest point above the stream and 404ft in length.

Continuing westwards towards Alnwick, and passing through another five cuttings, the next significant landmark was Shilbottle Sidings signalbox. The sidings at this small junction led into the gas works on its south side, while on the north side of the tracks were coal drops. Eventually, these coal drops became redundant due to the more convenient ones in the goods yard at Alnwick Station. The original coal drops area was later turned into an oil terminal under an agreement dated 9th June 1925. The signalbox was to have its name changed to Alnwick East, as Shilbottle Sidings became the name of the signalbox of the exchange sidings on the main line south of Wooden Gate around 1924, when connections to the new Shilbottle Colliery, owned by the Cooperative Wholesale Society, opened.

Situated just to the south-east of the railway bridge that crossed the A1 trunk road into Alnwick was the gas works, which supplied the town with coal gas for heating and lighting for many years. It had its own siding from the Alnwick Branch line where wagons of coal were brought on a regular basis to supply the retort house.

This new, improved gas works was created after considerable deliberation amongst the Alnwick Joint Stock Gas Company, the Duke of Northumberland and the Shilbottle Coal Company. Eventually, a Special Meeting of the Local Board of Health on 3rd December 1879 granted that a gas works be built at a cost of £9,894.

It had taken some considerable amount of time to plan and gain permission for lands to be used, as it crossed the original Shilbottle Colliery waggon-way. The land totalled three acres, three roods and thirty perches. Coal access to the works was a siding from the Alnwick branch railway line for which the Gas Company had to meet installation costs of £70. This siding left the branch line at Alnwick East signal box, formerly known as Shilbottle Sidings.

The three-acre site would have sufficient space for the retort house, two gas holders, three cottages and the manager's residence, and being close to both town and railway, would have the distinction of being "one of the most convenient gas works in the North of England".

Passing Alnwick East signalbox the branch ran directly into Alnwick, crossing over the busy Great North Road, under the bridge of Bridge Street, and into the station.

The town's residents now had a branch line that arrived near where the Shilbottle Colliery Railway first brought coals to Alnwick in 1809, this area of Alnwick becoming known as Waggonway Road as a result. The colliery's line fell short of the present day site, and terminated near South Road, from where a stone tramway was built to bring the coals the last half mile to the area where the NER built its coal drops. Waggonway Road became the site of the barracks for the workmen during the construction of the Cornhill branch during the late 1880s. These living quarters were locally known as "shanty charlies".

The Original Alnwick Station

Alnwick Station was originally built with very modest

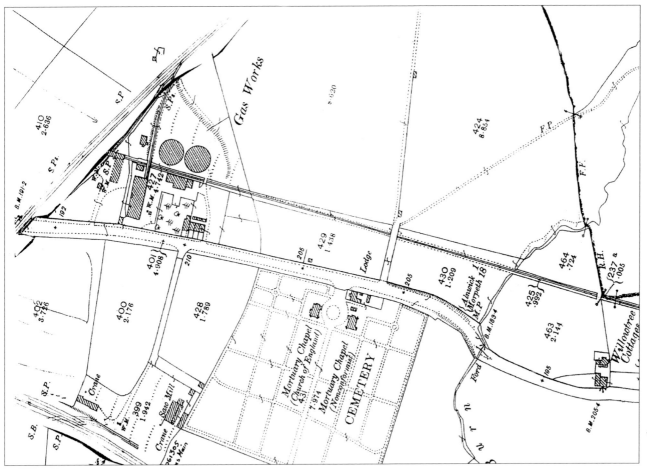

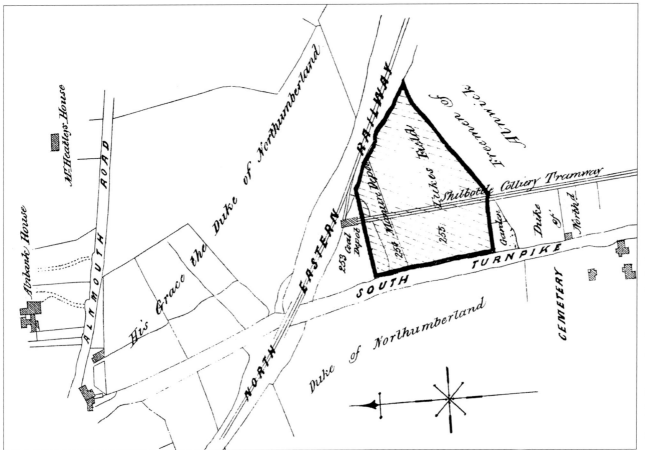

Alnwick Gasworks showing (left) the original 1878 proposal, and (right) as opened on 12th December 1882. (Reproduced by kind permission of the Ordnance Survey)

Top: *Shunting at Alnwick Gasworks, circa 1961. (R Breeze)*
Bottom: *Dundee's V2 60836, acquired from Tweedmouth, spent several weeks at Alnmouth as a temporary replacement for a K1 locomotive during April and May of 1966. Here it is on passenger duties between Alnmouth and Alnwick with a two coach train on the recently singled branch line. This locomotive became the last Gresley V2 locomotive to operate on British Railways, being withdrawn in December 1966. (SC Nash)*

Platform 1 of Alnwick station with the Coldstream train waiting inside the relatively new train shed around 1887. The view displays the wonderful arched roof and stonework of the building. (Aln Valley Railway Society)

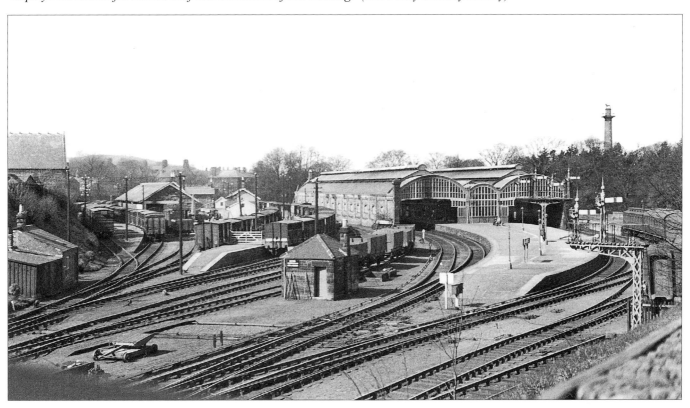

A panoramic scene of Alnwick station. The platform of the original station was used for goods traffic, and a gate was added to transform it into an unloading dock for cattle brought in for sale at the local markets. The small building towards the front is the weigh office. Not only are there three sidings full of cattle wagons, but a rake of early carriages stands in the sidings beside platform two. The Lion Tower dominates the background skyline. (Roger Carpenter, Duncan Wilcock Collection)

ALNWICK

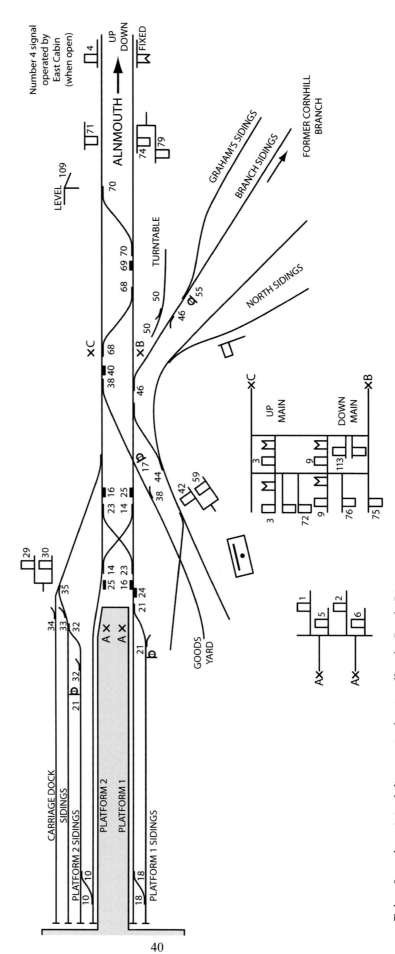

Taken from the original diagram in the signalbox by Bartle Rippon.

The early evening sunshine highlights the entrance to Alnwick station; the clock still remains in use today. To the left of the main archway is the Enquiry and Parcels Office, while to the right is the entrance created for WH Smith's bookshop. (John Mallon Collection)

Photographed many years later, on 30th May 2006, the main station building still maintains its imposing character. (Howard Sprenger/Kestrel Collection)

Above: The approaches to Alnwick showing the water tower, signal gantry, road bridge and signalbox circa 1961. (R Breeze)

Left: A similar view, taken from the turntable on 19th March 1966, the gantry now bereft of signals. (Ian S Carr)

top of this short incline was a decorative iron gate that allowed access on to the forecourt before entering the station building. The forecourt, with limited space, was rather simply but attractively designed. The ironwork used for the glazed canopy was of standard NER design with the Star of David motif in the supporting brackets. The large station clock that hung on the entrance wall was similar in make to the other clocks issued for the Cornhill line, and all were supplied by W Potts & Sons Ltd. Two clocks were purchased for the station at a cost of £12 10s 0d, and they still remain today in perfect working order, requiring winding only once a week.

Railway tickets were purchased from the booking office on the right hand side of the archway entrance for either platform one (trains to Wooler and Cornhill) or platform two (trains to Alnmouth, Newcastle and Edinburgh). Turning right towards platform one there was the booking office, the station master's office and the lamp room at the end. Beside the lamp room and the platform edge was the barrier entrance for platform one with the ticket collector's office, which became the cleaners' room at a later date.

The platform buildings were positioned along the centre of the island platform where there was the general waiting room and the first and third class ladies' rooms, with their respective toilets sandwiched in between. There was then an archway connecting platform one and platform two, and next followed the first class gentlemen's room. The remaining two stone-built rooms were used for the boilers and the gents' toilets respectively. Attached to the end of the gents' toilets was a wooden structure used as the refreshment room, which was added around 1897. The exact date appears to be unknown, although the refreshment room was constructed sometime after an article appeared in *The Alnwick Wasp* of April 1892: "A meeting of the inhabitants of Alnwick will be held at an early date and the question of having refreshment rooms at the new railway station will be considered. Luke, Lack and Bush will then state their opinions." A bookstall also occupied some space near the refreshment room but its position is not exactly known.

The boiler room was constructed for heating foot-warmers, and supplying them to the passengers of the trains as no heating was available in early passenger carriages. The heated foot-warmers would be passed through a small hatch from the boiler room and into the waiting trains. As passenger coach design improved in comfort, steam-heating systems were introduced, eliminating the need for foot-warmers.

Turning left after entering the main entrance was the parcels office with the porters' room in the corner of the building, and from here passengers went through the barriers on to platform one. The original booking office was eventually moved and incorporated within the parcels office during 1938, allowing WH Smith to use the original ticket office, with a little alteration, as their bookshop.

The magnificent two-arched roof spanned each of the tracks, with a smaller arch over the platform itself. Each of the large spans was 38ft 10in wide, while the smaller middle one was 17ft 3in. Built mostly of timber, there were glass panels used at the uppermost part of the roof and the south-facing platform ends, which allowed sunlight to penetrate to the platforms. These would, through time, discolour from the smoke emitted by the steam locomotives.

To the immediate south of the station, a large signalbox was erected to replace the original one. The new box was a 3-storey structure, giving a more commanding vision over the top of the bridge and further along both approach lines from Alnmouth and Wooler, as well as superb views of all departing trains in and out of both station and goods yard.

Beyond the new station and past the signalbox was a 50-foot turntable supplied by Cowans and Sheldon in 1887 at a cost of £327, and numbered 1590. This was situated between the lines branching eastwards to Alnmouth and southwards to Cornhill (Coldstream). It remained until 1967, not long before the railway's demise. A water column was also added near to the turntable, being a parachute type column also built by Cowans and Sheldon (No 1127). It had a capacity of 2,000 gallons, and drew its supply from the town's water system. It would be dismantled at the same time as the turntable.

No expense appears to have been spared in the newer construction, as there were five signalboxes to control train movements around the Alnwick area. They were at Willowburn, Shilbottle Colliery Junction, Station Junction, Alnwick North and Summit. Alnwick North, Willowburn and Summit all ended their days following the complete closure of the Cornhill line.

Passenger Services

Alnwick was a busy place during the late 1800s and early 1900s, with a regular passenger service to Alnmouth, including two of the morning services continuing to Newcastle, a frequent goods service operating and the arrival of excursion trains. The branch line was being well used with up to 60 trains a day using the station. Ken Hoole states that in 1901, ticket sales at Alnwick amounted to 55,359.

The passenger rolling stock used on the Alnwick and Cornhill branch lines comprised NER four- and six-wheeled stock. It was the standard stock for the NER, and could be found throughout the region. The carriages were built around the 1880s and 1890s, or even earlier, and could be rather uncomfortable to travel on. Some fine examples of these carriages exist today as part of the preserved Tanfield Railway line in County Durham. They have been carefully restored to their former state, although running with newer chassis and wheels.

During the early Victorian period of the railway, Alnwick shopkeepers would ask customers if they were going home by train. If so, an errand boy would deliver the goods to the waiting party on board the departing train. One record from *Rail Tales and Station Stories* tells of an errand boy who walked along the side of the waiting departure train shouting for the attention of the person who had bought a parcel. As there was no answer, the errand boy threw the parcel through an open window where it landed on a passenger's lap. The passenger protested that he was not the recipient to which the errand boy replied, "Well you are now!" and proceeded to run off. At that point the whistle blew and the train departed the station!

Gradually, both passenger and goods traffic increased until 45 passenger trains were operating each way between Alnmouth and Alnwick by 1911. In 1932, the Alnwick and Alnmouth to Newcastle trains were worked using five "Composition A" sets comprising two brake third-class coaches, one composite lavatory coach and one third-class composite coach. The coaches would be used on other local trips in between their visits to Alnwick. The Alnwick and Alnmouth to Berwick trains that served the intermediate stations on the main line between Alnmouth and Berwick used three "Composition C" sets made up of two brake composites, each with first-class compartments, according to the carriage roster.

During the 1930s, LNER corridor coaches were drafted in to replace the NER bogie compartment stock that was more than twenty years old. It was the shortage of corridor brake coaches that caused the use of non-corridor stock following World War II, where Pullman third-class coaches were used on the Newcastle to Alnwick passenger service for a short period of time.

The Alnwick, Coldstream and Tweedmouth parcels train was an interesting working. It was a six-wheeled van that was rostered to depart Newcastle at 6.53am attached to the Berwick parcels train, and was then left at Alnmouth *en-route*. At Alnmouth, it was transferred to Alnwick, where it travelled to Coldstream as a No 1 braked parcels train, but by 1939 it had become classed as a No 1 express parcels train!

It is believed that during the summer period, passengers were taken to the camping coaches situated along the line at Whittingham, Glanton, Hedgley, Wooperton, Ilderton, Akeld, Kirknewton and Mindrum by this service. This train appears to have been exclusively for occupiers of the camping coaches, as there is no mention of the train in the passenger workings lists.

As the new diesel multiple units first appeared on the Newcastle to Alnwick trains on 14th April 1958, the older rolling stock and steam locomotives started to become redundant. By the end of the 1950s, for instance, all the LNER class D20 4-4-0 locomotives at Alnmouth engine shed had been withdrawn, and sold for scrap.

Excursion Traffic

Alnwick became a popular venue for day excursions, particularly from Tyneside, and until 1908 the old station platform became known as the excursion platform before it was eventually converted for use as a cattle dock. Ken Hoole states that the passenger trains were made up of four- and six-wheeled NER coaches, and that by 1898, the maximum allowed for any excursion was twenty. This usually entailed double-heading if the train exceeded twelve carriages. At the time, the assisting locomotive could be added either to the

front or back of the train, but within a few years, the practice was altered to having the locomotive attached to the front of the train.

Excursions from the north (for example, Wooler) were allowed nine four-wheeled coaches if hauled by a passenger locomotive, or eleven if hauled by a goods locomotive. Six-wheeled coaches were limited to nine if hauled by a goods locomotive. The maximum number of coaches allowed on the Cornhill line was eleven. Alnwick was unique as a branch line, as virtually any class of locomotive could arrive at the station on specials and excursions.

Loads of ordinary and excursion trains, 1908

Class	Alnmouth to Alnwick		Alnwick to Alnmouth	
	No of vehicles	Load (Tons)	No of vehicles	Load (Tons)
M1, Q	14	196	16	224
A, C1, F1, I, J, 901, 1463	11	134	15	210
O and Goods (ordinary train)	14	196	16	224
O and Goods (excursion train)	16	224	20	280
Maximum load with assistance	20	280	27	378

In the *Alnwick and County Gazette and Guardian*, July to September 1939, an advert appeared offering luxurious travel in the "Tourist Stock" coaches for a trip to Blackpool on Monday 25th September 1939. The train was planned to leave at 6.30am, arriving in Blackpool at 1.00pm the same day. The excursion would then depart at 11pm the same evening, and arrive at Alnwick at 6.15am the following day. However, an advert appeared on 8th September notifying of the train's cancellation stating: "In view of hostilities and the prevailing conditions in the country, we have had to cancel our September Monday excursion. We take this opportunity to thank all our readers who have booked to travel with us, and apologize for the disappointment that has been caused by this unavoidable decision". (*Rail Tales and Station Stories*)

Goods Work

During the early 1900s, both passenger and goods traffic was quite considerable. In 1911, passenger ticket sales amounted to 77,771 according to the Aln Valley Railway Society website, while 2,394 tons of building stone and 1,754 tons of grain were despatched from Alnwick, and 1,380 wagons of livestock were loaded.

Top: Class V2 2-6-2 60836 departing Alnwick on the 4.32pm for Alnmouth in May 1966. (John Newbegin)
Bottom: Class K1 2-6-0 62006 departs for Alnmouth sometime in early 1966. (John Newbegin)

Class V2 60836 arrives at Alnwick in May 1966 (top) and, below, K1 62011 leaves in March 1966. (Both John Newbegin)

52

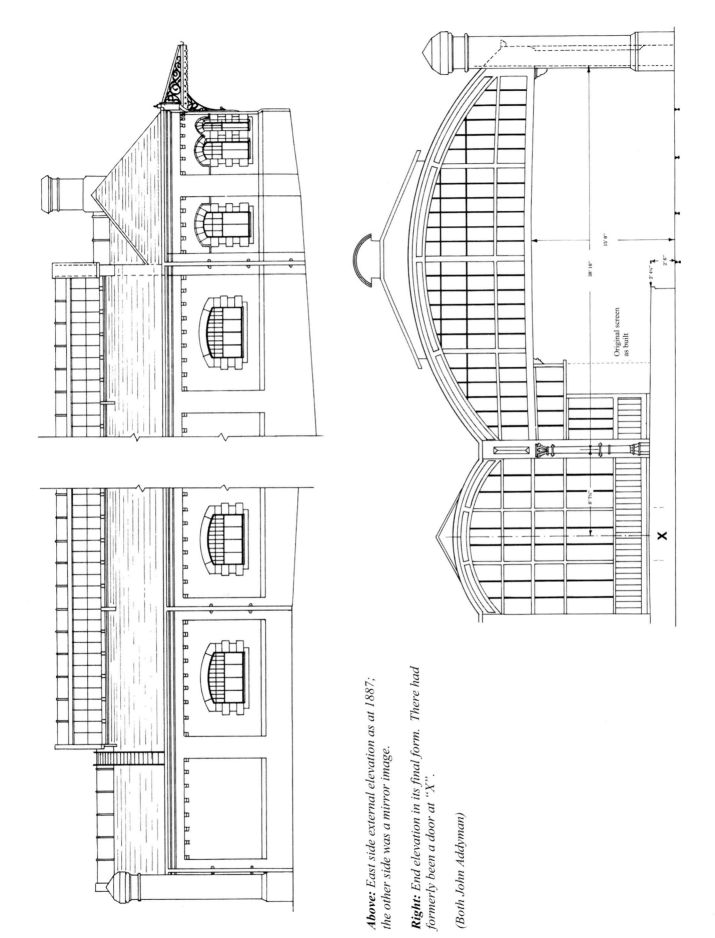

Above: East side external elevation as as at 1887;
the other side was a mirror image.

Right: End elevation in its final form. There had
formerly been a door at "X".

(Both John Addyman)

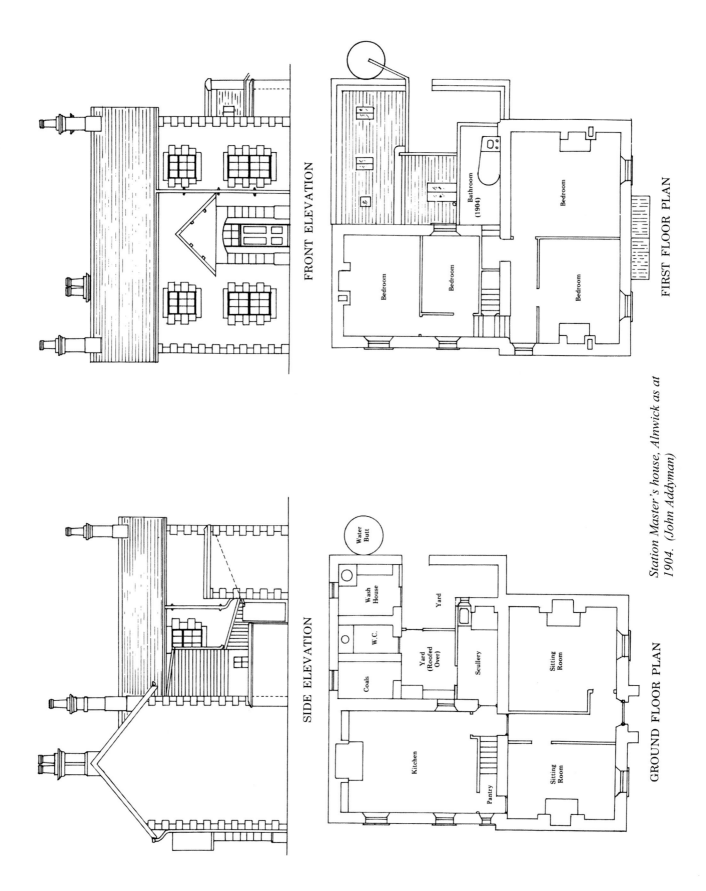

FRONT ELEVATION

SIDE ELEVATION

FIRST FLOOR PLAN

Bedroom

Bathroom
(1904)

Bedroom

Bedroom

Bedroom

GROUND FLOOR PLAN

Wash
House

W.C.

Coals

Yard

Yard
(Roofed
Over)

Scullery

Sitting
Room

Kitchen

Pantry

Sitting
Room

Water
Butt

*Station Master's house, Alnwick as at
1904. (John Addyman)*

72

Accidents, Mishaps and Unusual Events

Derailments were not a regular occurrence but were certainly not uncommon. The Alnmouth locomotives were involved on several occasions, and included here are some extracts that happened over the years.

Alnmouth's most noted locomotive accident was the crash at Chevington Station 25th October 1887, involving the Amble Branch passenger train. Whilst going to collect two cattle wagons to add to the passenger train for Amble, a southbound goods train failed to stop at the danger signals. It rammed into the passenger train, pushing it into the cattle train waiting to have its two cattle wagons removed. The Chevington station master was killed, and much damage to both locomotives and wagons occurred. It is not known if there were any people aboard the Amble passenger train at the time, or whether any livestock was in the wagons. A detailed account of events is told in *Signals to Danger* by JA Wells.

In his book, *North Eastern Branch Line Termini*, Ken Hoole reports that on 11th November 1898, the 8.50pm Alnwick to Alnmouth train succumbed to an unusual accident when it was misdirected on to the wrong line. The driver misread the signals, and was unaware that the train was on the down line until it came upon some catch points. These were required in the track in order to derail any runaway vehicles. The engine was running bunker first when it left the rails and ended up on its side. No-one was seriously injured, although it was reported that the driver fell on top of the fireman, who was busily sweeping the cab floor. The locomotive suffered only superficial damage, while the leading coach turned on its side and the other three derailed. Of the few travelling passengers only one complained of injury while the guard was "hurt on the head".

During January 1948, a goods train was standing on the up main line taking water from the water column at the south end of the station. While it was quenching its thirst, a following goods train coming from the Longhoughton direction failed to stop at the danger signals, and ploughed into the back of the stationary train. The main line was closed for several hours while the debris was cleared, and a mountain of potatoes collected as the stationary train was taking a load of seed potatoes to the southern markets. Perhaps some local railway workers benefited from "free" seedlings, and reaped the rewards the following summer. (*Rail Tales and Station Stories*)

In March 1956, class J39 64924, was derailed while entering the station at Alnwick. The Tweedmouth crane was summoned to do the rerailing, and the tender removed, but while the locomotive was being lifted, it slipped and fell onto its side, causing even greater difficulty putting her back on the rails. The locomotive was rerailed later that day.

A year later, a similar occurrence happened with class V1 2-6-2T 67646 as it too became derailed entering the station. The Tweedmouth breakdown crane was more successful this time.

Around this time the saddest of occurences happened when a railway worker, who was preparing to couple together some moving wagons, slipped, was crushed and died between the buffers of the rolling stock. No date is given for this sad accident, but it occurred sometime during the early 1950s. (*Rail Tales and Station Stories*)

The Tweedmouth breakdown crane arrived at Alnmouth on 6th October 1963 behind locomotive A3 pacific 60040, *Cameronian*. On its arrival at Alnmouth, I made a note that the locomotive had to run around its train, and then proceeded on its journey to Alnwick travelling tender first – a strange sight watching a large Gresley passenger locomotive travelling backwards with its breakdown train. I was later informed by the Alnmouth station staff that the pilot engine, class K1 62021, had been derailed while it was performing its shunting duties.

A more unusual sight was noted by John Newbegin, who briefly worked as a signal lad on leaving school in August 1966. He wrote an article for *The Link*, the magazine of the Aln Valley Railway Society, regarding a photograph showing Deltic locomotive 9004, *Queen's Own Highlander*, at Alnwick with a breakdown crane from Gateshead during July 1966. As all steam locomotives had gone from the region, the goods workings were operated by Clayton type 1 diesels, and while shunting in the goods yard one of these had become derailed.

Unusual Events – Robbery

Not everyone was of good character, as *Rail Tales and Station Stories* tells of a robbery committed at Alnwick Station. The following report in the *Alnwick and County Gazette* for Saturday 24th August 1889 states:

Alleged Robbery in a Railway Carriage

At Alnwick Petty Sessions, Elizabeth Lamb, 31, single woman and a ladies' attendant at the waiting rooms, Bilton Junction, was appearing having been charged with stealing a purse containing £3 6s from a bag in a railway carriage at Alnwick station, the property of Peter Pavester Bosumworth, foreman over the lamp department at the NER works at Gateshead, on the 6th of the present month. Miss Lamb claimed she found the purse lying at the bottom of the railway carriage. The arresting officer, PC Dixon, had brought her from her lodgings at Bilton to Alnwick and locked her up. She was formally charged with the offence, and pleaded not guilty. She was committed for trial at Northumberland Quarter Sessions. Bail was accepted in two sureties of £5 each and herself in £10.

A second robbery reported in *Rail Tales and Station*

Stories occurred many years later, and was reported as "The Little Train Robbery":

Shortly after World War II, an incident occurred when the last train arrived at Alnmouth on its way to Alnwick from Newcastle, and all the passengers had dispersed. There was one person sitting on the platform seat, so Willie, the guard, asked him if he was getting on the train. Replying that he wasn't, but was only waiting for his brother who had obviously missed the train, he said that he would remain seated in the hope of his arrival. The train left for Alnwick, and on its return, Willie noticed that this person had disappeared and thought no more about it. The following day when Willie got to work there was a tremendous amount of fuss about a robbery. A goods van containing a load of cigarettes had been waiting at Alnmouth to be taken to Alnwick for the local businesses. On its arrival at Alnwick the seals of the van were removed, only to find a wooden crate and no cigarettes. When the police arrived at the scene and began to examine it, sawdust was seen around the crate, and on moving the crate, they found a hole large enough for a man to get in. On further investigation parcel tickets had been altered by a railway clerk in Newcastle, and with the aid of accomplices, the consignment of cigarettes had been stolen. The clerk and the accomplices were subsequently arrested for stealing.

A German Invasion?

During the summer of 1971, I was taken by surprise when a film crew arrived at Alnmouth Station one afternoon. Being naturally inquisitive, I asked the station staff what was going on, and was told by Joe Miller, the office clerk, that they were there to film a scene for a forthcoming television programme about two World War II army sergeants "on the run" in Germany. The film action was taking place at the end of the truncated branch where three wagons had been specially placed.

As the crew and actors assembled on the platform, out of the waiting room appeared a very tall actor in a German uniform. This immense-looking figure suddenly surprised me, and I then realised what a German soldier must have really looked like. Quite frightening! Everyone disappeared along the branch line to film the scene, and that was the last I saw of them for the remainder of the day. I never did find out the end result!

The Railway Mural at Barter Books, Alnwick station. Designed by Mary Manley, founder of Barter Books, the mural lists the names of all known staff from 1850 to 1960 in alphabetical order, with the Station Masters' names being picked out in red. The design also includes the coats-of-arms of the three railway companies that were in operation during the station's working life, the North Eastern Railway, the London and North Eastern Railway and British Railways. The mural was formally opened on 5th September 2005, 118 years to the day after the opening of the new station at Alnwick.
(Reproduced by kind permission of Barter Books)

Appendix B

Station Masters

This information has been obtained from Government Censuses between 1851 and 1901, the Ken Hoole Study Centre, Darlington Museum and Barter Books.

All effort has been made to give the correct information – apologies for any missing names.

Alnwick Station

1851   James Rutherford
1861   Francis Morrell
1881   Robert Taylor
1887   John Patterson
1902   John Carlisle
1919   George Charlton
1924   EK Cowen
1933   Robert Reid
1950   OC Sim
1955   Alfred Middleton

Alnmouth Station

1861   John Taylor
1871   John Taylor
1881   John Taylor
1891   William Hardie
1901   Joseph Walton
1914   T Short
1920   Henry Defty
1928   William Scarth
1934   AG Minty
1937   CJ Lamb
1938   WH Mather
1940   NA Liddell
1946   G Brown
1951   FG Dolby
1964   AS Lee
1965   RS Burrell

Alnmouth station staff in 1920. Back row, from left: Frederick Weddell (Clerk), Matthew Kean, Ralph Albert Patterson (Porter - Goods), unknown, Robert Straughan, Harold Carlisle (Clerk). Middle row: Robert Patrick (Clerk), unknown, Stephen Griffiths (Porter/Guard), Thomas Charlton (Station Foreman), Thomas Punton, Edward Redpath, Walter Harrison. Front row: Isabela Smith (Office Cleaner), Elizabeth Defty (Clerk), Henry Defty (SM), Amy Watson (Refreshment Room Attendant). (Defty Family/John Mallon Collection)

Example Train Recordings

An example of the many train recordings made by the author while train-spotting at Alnmouth station. These sightings were made on 19th August, 1963. Total trains recorded: 41 (Steam: 13, Deltics: 9)

Locomotive No	Train	Time	Through or Stopping	Direction	Remarks
D9005	Passenger	09.20	Through	Up	
60005	Passenger	09.45	Stopping	Down	
D250	Passenger	09.50	Stopping	Down	
D353	Goods	09.55	Through	Down	
D9019	Passenger	10.10	Through	Up	
62021	Goods	10.10	Through	Down	
60052	Goods	10.30	Through	Down	
61221	Goods	10.50		Up	To up yard
60954	Light	11.00	Through	Up	
D9006	Passenger	11.25	Through	Up	*Flying Scotsman*
60020	Goods	11.30	Through	Down	
D245	Passenger	11.40	Through	Down	
D394	Goods	11.55	Through	Up	
D385	Passenger	12.00	Through	Down	*North Briton*
D1520	Passenger	12.30	Through	Up	
D352	Passenger	12.35	Stopping	Up	
D9012	Passenger	12.45	Through	Down	
62023	Goods	12.50		Down	To down yard
62006	Light	12.52		Down	To down yard
D273	Passenger	13.05	Through	Up	AS car carrier
D363	Passenger	13.10	Through	Down	AS car carrier
D399	Passenger	13.20	Through	Up	*Queen of Scots*
60904	Goods	13.20	Through	Down	
D260	Goods	13.30	Through	Down	
DMU	Passenger	14.15	Stopping	Up	E56218, E50231
D393	Goods	14.30	Through	Up	
D9013	Passenger	14.45	Through	Down	*Flying Scotsman*
D9008	Passenger	15.05	Through	Up	
DP2	Passenger	15.05	Through	Down	Experimental locomotive
63381	Goods	15.08	Through	Down	
D242	Goods	15.45	Through	Up	
D387	Goods	15.50	Through	Down	
D9004	Passenger	16.30	Through	Down	
D250	Passenger	16.45	Stopping	Up	
60940	Goods	17.10	Through	Down	
D9012	Passenger	17.15	Through	Down	
60952	Passenger	17.15	Through	Up	
63381	Light	17.40	Through	Up	
D393	Light	17.40	Through	Down	
D359	Light	17.55	Through	Up	
D9007	Passenger	18.00	Through	Down	*Queen of Scots*

Queen of Scots Pullman cars:
Up, 8 cars: 79, 80, 350, 358, *Garnet, Robin, Eagle*, 352.
Down, 7 cars: 71, 332, *Hawk, Nilar, Emerald*, 348, 77.